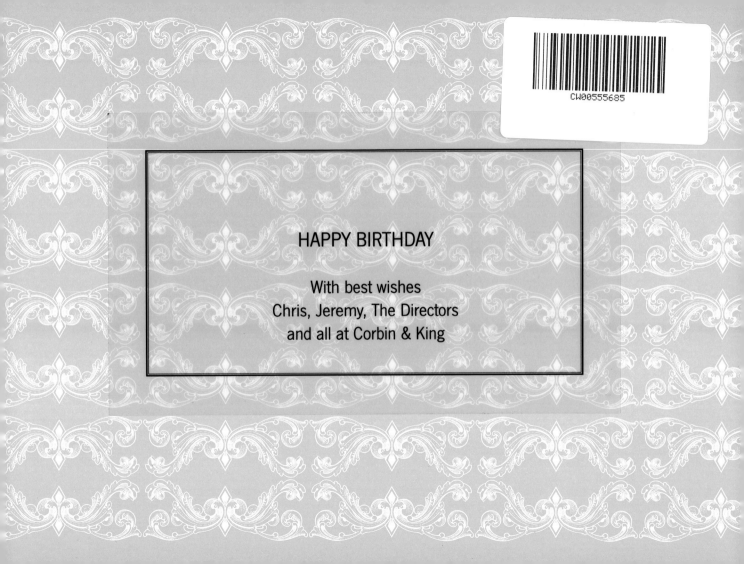

HAPPY BIRTHDAY

With best wishes
Chris, Jeremy, The Directors
and all at Corbin & King

quadrille

A. A. GILL

BRASSERIE
ZÉDEL

TRADITIONS *and* RECIPES

FROM A GRAND BRASSERIE

PHOTOGRAPHS BY DAVID LOFTUS   RECIPES BY ANDREW PARKINSON

~BIENVENUE~

Brasserie Zédel is the evocation of the most opulent and expansive of all cafés: the Grand Café.

If a questing tourist were to ask you where the heart of London could be found, you would probably tug the brim of your costermonger's bowler, stick a knowing thumb in your waistcoat pocket and reply 'The old town's strawberry? Lor' love us guv!' Why you can feel its beat under the cobbles; hear it in the chimes of St Paul's and the bells of Fortnum's servile clock; see it in the yellow light of a London cab thrumming on a midnight street on a wet Wednesday. It's in the scarlet coat of a Chelsea Pensioner explaining his medals to a bemused

GRILL ROOM, REGENT PALACE HOTEL, PICCADILLY, W.1.

The brasserie as originally built in the 1920s

KITCHEN, REGENT PALACE HOTEL, PICCADILLY CIRCUS, W. I.

The original brasserie kitchen

Norwegian au pair. London's heart steams in Her Majesty's horse-poo on The Mall. It rings out from Nelson's tin chest and in every pigeon that's called this dear old window home.

If your interlocuteur – not being a poetic man – rather literally insists on being given directions, you would probably point him to Piccadilly Circus. Though a cartographer would say that the centre of London, the point where Dick Whittington's milestones are measured from, is the Cross at Charing – one of twelve erected to mark the resting places of the body of Edward I's Queen as she made her sombre way to the Abbey for burial. In fact the name 'Charing' may come from *chère reine* meaning 'dear Queen', though to be utterly pedantic and correct (and what would be the point of a cartographer who wasn't), the exact spot of the original cross is where Charles I now sits on the finest bronze horse in London at the edge of Trafalgar Square. That is where measurements to London are taken from and

it's always *to*, never *from*. Leaving London is a journey measured in regret not distance. But still Piccadilly would seem to be your best bet, not least because it has always been where young visitors have paused to sit and consider whatever it is the young consider in the caravanserai of youth.

Piccadilly seems to mark the meeting point of the constituent parts of London, the loucheness of slurred literary Soho, the retail city on Regent Street, the gaiety of theatreland starting at Charing Cross Road. To the south, clubbable, counting house, establishment London, and Piccadilly is where daytime London meets the night. It is the city's social meridian and the presence of Eros implies affairs of the heart. Although again, to be slavishly Malvolioish about it, Waterhouse's statue (one of the very few made from aluminium) is not Eros at all but the lad's younger brother Anteros. You can always tell him from his sibling by his odd hybrid propulsion system – feathered butterfly wings. Anteros is 'returned love', 'reciprocal love', 'love that grows from love'. In this particular case the love of Lord Shaftesbury for the poor. But it could also be the echo, the flash, the glimmer of the abiding or transient love we feel for the city and the animistic belief that even if she doesn't show it and would be loathe to admit it, London loves us back. And finally, if the tourist asked for a recommendation as to where they should eat, the Londoner would be stumped. Piccadilly is a great smörgåsbord, a medieval market of the savourily unsavoury, the gastrically challenging various begged and borrowed constructions of international carbohydrate combined with things that are minced and stewed beyond recognition, coated in sugar, salt, fat and vinegar; the polyglot taste of cheap food all designed specifically to be consumed in a shorter time than it takes the consumer to have sex and all prepared with the certain knowledge that none of these customers will ever return. It is the cuisine that is globally and universally known as 'tourist food'. Wherever you find it, tourist food will be familiar, badly made from poor ingredients, coarsely flavoured and carelessly served. It is a contrary truth that if a stranger from a strange land were your guests at home you would serve them the best you had... made with care and offered with self-deprecating exclamations on your grandmother's crockery. But we give visitors to our city whatever we think we can get away with and charge whatever the unwary will swallow. Tourist food is a civic embarrassment and we tell people to avoid it; and when we travel, these same people tell us to avoid it. It remains the most ubiquitous food avoided by everyone at the same time and eaten by everyone. Tourist food is the oldest cuisine in the world after home cooking. Tourist food is the original public catering: the pie man and the whelk stall, the hand-held pasty seller, the purveyors of buns and puddings that stuffed a hole in hungry travellers were all tourist food.

If you yearn to know what the Middle Ages ate in the ancient city, then just eat anywhere around Piccadilly Circus where the preparation is done in the window. A doner kebab after eight pints of beer is more authentically Plantagenet than anything you'll see at the Royal Shakespeare Company. And if by now your impatient tourist is still loitering for a practical answer, you could always slap your head and say 'of course, I know where you should go… you must eat at Brasserie Zédel'.

You could easily pass Zédel without noticing. It's not in hiding or purposefully obscure, it's just not blousy or flashy or loud. It has a petite elegance about it. And though you might miss it, you might just as easily find it by serendipity (always the best tour guide). You'll be looking in shop windows and voilà! You'll be surprised by the familiar but unlikely savoir-faire of a little café that sits behind delicate little tables on the pavement. Through the windows encrypted with the gold lettering of pre-neon advertising you can see a small bar. Newspapers on sticks, walls thick with interest, and you'll think 'this is the little bar…', the café the travellers always tell you they found like a treasure. 'We found this little place', they say. '…It was perfect.' The perfect little place. You know the one. The one you always hope to find amongst the authentic tourist offerings. And you could go and sit and have a beer there or a *citron pressé* and read *Le Monde* and look back out of the window at the bustle and swagger, and then you could pay your bill and leave thinking, 'What a great find'. Or, you could linger and notice that a lot of people walk through the café, past the little bar, and never come back. Is this the front for some secret religion? Is the café's toilet eating people? The café on the street is actually the wardrobe you pass through to get into a French Narnia. This is the wings to the great proscenium below. It is a tease, an *amuse bouche* ahead of the big reveal. Go further and you'll walk into a broad corridor, down a sashaying staircase and into a foyer, the walls hung with French theatrical posters from last century. There is a racy mural of planes and boats and trains and a time traveller's sense that you might have stepped into the première of a Maurice Chevalier film, or be about to steam across the Channel. There is a smiling hat-check girl in her booth and a choice of doorways. For the sake of drama, you walk through the one straight ahead of you.

Contemporary restaurants tend to be short of wow. We have become blasé about the drama of dining. We assume that they are going to try to impress and semaphore their unique pleasures. There is still plenty of 'oh!' but very little 'wow'. Zédel's opening number is a big, big 'ta-dah'! You know you're in a basement. You know because you've walked downstairs from the street, *ipso facto* Watson, we are in the cellar! But here is an enormous room with vast ceilings and cathedral windows. It is so unlike any other cellar, basement, bunker, crypt or catacomb you've ever been in that for a moment it makes you doubt your altimeter. This, in short – and in long – is a very, very grand room with huge Corinthian pillars and blooming golden finials. There's a long bar and dozens of soigné tables set with linen and napery; there are waiters in black and white who glide with silver trays. This dining room hums. Purrs with the excited, contented continuo that is the choir of lunch, the generator of hospitality.

All restaurants are born in Utopia. Someone sitting in a kitchen says, 'What if we made the perfect hamburger bar, souvlaki stall, date restaurant – the most glittering plutocratic, snobbish, socially insecure dining room ever?'.

Jeremy King and Chris Corbin have made more successful trips to catering Utopia than almost any other restaurateurs. They have blaséd material dreams at Le Caprice, The Ivy, J. Sheekey, The Wolseley, The Delaunay, Colbert, Fischer's and

Bellanger. They practise a particularly austere and extreme form of restaurant reverie – they don't just dream a dream, they are 'method' restaurateurs imagining not simply a room as a set with a menu as a script, but the history of the characters who made it. I've had conversations with Jeremy about people, occasions and places that only exist in his imagination. He'll find old photographs of the folk who started this imagined restaurant he's inventing; mementos from their holidays, examples of their hobbies. He'll know the names of their children, the waitresses they seduced… and then had to pay for the trouble with their first wives. He'll know the hand in the poker game that won enough money to buy the suit that got them their first job as a waiter in a Viennese café. He'll be able to tell you about the day Mistinguett came and danced on the table and when the Prince of Wales was turned away by a maître d' who thought he was a fat Irishman. He will explain why certain dishes on the menu are important because they were made by someone's imaginary grandmother or remind them of some made-up home they had to leave as refugees. This presentation of place is no dinner party game, no exercise that simply grows into an anecdote – neither is it a snapshot. It is a process that expands and collects the barnacles of teaspoons, recipes, matchbooks, cryptic messages on napkins until slowly the fiction is transformed into a carapace of fact. The tables, chairs, engraved glass, tiled floor, the artfully stopped clock, a barman, a manager, a doorman, grill, a chocolate room, handmade coffee pots that have to be just so, a napkin that's big enough for a stout man with a Clemenceau moustache to tuck into his detachable collar and not drip onion soup on his Italian silk waistcoat – will become real. Tangible. A place the rest of us can sit and wonder.

This story – this creation myth – can and does appear to drive the more practical artisans of construction to sheer eye-rolling exasperation.

Hotel Ritz

Simone de Beauvoir at Les Deux Magots

It can seem wearily extreme but the process is fascinating as the constantly discussed fiction grows corporeal in front of your eyes, until the room is born confident with a back story and a heritage and the unwitting regulars arrive at the restaurant they've never seen before feeling they've been coming all their lives.

You could mock this process if it hadn't been so successful. King and Corbin are the most imitated and respected restaurateurs in a city that knows how to eat out. Zédel was transported here by a triumph of levitating imagination, but it also came carrying an older, longer and even grander story.

Zédel is French. A French café. A grand French café with a brasserie menu. And if your ever-persistent tourist asks why he should visit a French café in London, you might mention that it is almost certainly better than visiting an English café in London – and that anyway, you'll have difficulty finding an English café. Cafés from the Grand to the kiosk are more often than not run by immigrants; not just in England, but everywhere. The café is the simplest and cheapest small business to start as an entry into a new home. You use your family as staff, a husband cooks and the wife takes the money or vice versa. The café is not specifically technically a French invention. Vienna and Venice both vie for the honour of the first European caf, though each imported or stole the idea from Turkey and the Muslim world where cafés were men-only affairs for chaps to talk religion and politics and sip the sweet, strong, thick coffee that Yemenis brought out of Ethiopia. But all over the world our idea of a café is French. The Grand Café – the Café Lux – was a particularly French invention. Having come up with the concept of the restaurant at the turn of the nineteenth century, the new sophisticated and Bohemian urban class needed somewhere to go to be sophisticated with other Bohemians.

When I was first taken to Paris by my father at the age of 13 it was the year after the great youth-quake of 1968. As the Soviet tanks rolled over the velvet revolution in Prague, so the streets of Paris became a battleground of student protest and a fog of exclamatory Utopian rhetoric. A year later the cobblestones still stood in piles and the riot police hung in bored huddles, smoking up alleys looking at girls' bottoms. This was still a Paris that smelt of *pissoirs* and Gitanes. It was dirty and it was beautiful, with all those tense contradictions that make French culture irresistible and infuriating – both sacred and profane, coarse and elegant, intelligent and imbecilic, rude and ruder.

In the *jolie laide* city it was cafés that were the great revelation – so different from grey London. The pavements and dark bars were still full of students waving their hands, flicking their hair, rolling their eyes and insouciantly wringing the last drop of dogma from the glorious failure of their rebellion. This was still the Paris of Sartre and Gainsbourg, Truffaut and Picasso. At the Brasserie Lipp we sat and ate moules next to Cabinet ministers, film stars and ladies of an unknown vintage dressed in Chanel feeding pâté to tiny poodles. Cafés in all their shapes and sizes were where life happened, where people make politics, made business, made art and advances. I'd never seen so many people kiss in public as I did in Paris. Not the platform back-to-school kisses of home, but big-screen, gasping, save-my-life kissing. The sort of kissing you had to learn or practise, that thing my grandmother most deeply despises – public displays of affection. If you asked where the heart of Paris was a Frenchman would probably pretend not to understand you and then point to the nearest café. The other thing my grandmother despises was eating in public. Paris celebrated both kissing and chewing.

Of course life happens everywhere, but what was mesmerising about cafés was that it happened as a sort of theatre. It was like taking the back off a watch and seeing the cogs turn and springs flex – this was the mechanics of culture and society with coffee and croissant. In '68 it was a knowing, very Gallic understanding that what was happening here was a repetition of a long shadow from history – the Paris commune of 1871. The setting for Victor Hugo's *Les Misérables* after the terrible humiliating defeat of the Franco-Prussian war which France had declared because of some diplomatic affront, and that ended with the bombardment of a starving Paris and a lot of students declaring a communal government of the people for a brief, brave idealistic moment.

One of the things that the French Grand Café gave the world was Russian service, in itself brought to France by emigrants from the East, all of whom claimed to be counts and princes who had been ousted by kulaks and Communists. They became waiters and tall-story tellers, depressives, drunks and ultimately homesick, bedsit suicides. Russian service is the easiest and most efficient way of getting food from pan to plate to punter for restaurants. Confusingly, French service is now rarely used except in carveries – it is when the food is all laid out at once, either down the centre of a table or down a sideboard. Diners help themselves with the help of butlers. French service is essentially for banquets and dinners in private houses where everyone is eating the same food. There is also *service anglais*, which in England is called silver service. A waiter balancing a salver on his left hand serves with a fork and spoon manipulated in his right hand. He serves a seated diner from their left side. Butler service is a variation on this where the diner helps themselves from the dish held by the waiter and is almost always reserved for private lunches or dinners. With Russian service the table is laid with the flatware – knives, forks, spoons, a plate and napkin. The waiter brings the food either plated or like silver service in the kitchen. I know that you often lie awake worrying about which fork to use... I know this because it's commonly said in newspapers and films and literary fiction, to show the anxiety of the lowly-born being introduced into high society. As in the apocryphal story of Edith Piaf and the Prince of Wales. Just on the chance one of you hasn't heard it before – Piaf, nervously at dinner with the English m'lord thinks her finger bowl is the soup and starts to drink it. The rest of the table smirks at her uncouth *faux pas*. The prince picks up his spoon and starts to eat his finger bowl. The rest of the party, chastened and socially trumped, are forced to follow suit and eat not only their finger bowls but humble pie as well. This story illustrates the difference between etiquette and manners. As I'm sure you know, etiquette is what the French have, manners is what the English have. The etiquette sniggered at the girl for not knowing the rules, the manners were putting her at her ease.

The answer to the great cutlery quiz is – start from the outside and work your way in toward the plate. It is no more complex than that. If it were, the upper classes would never have managed it. If it doesn't work, it's the fault of whoever laid the table who didn't know what they were doing, or who comes from Turkey, where I'm told they do it all differently. Alternatively, pick up whatever you fancy and eat the peas off your knife, because no one is watching – and if they are, it isn't because of your silverware dexterity. I'm also told that provincial hostesses worry to the point of alopecia about whether or not pudding spoons ought to be put above the plate or if this is in fact a raised pinky faux-genteelism, like antimacassars or standing up when the Queen appears on the television. Well it isn't. It is particularly English, along with napkin rings and cheese knives with curled-up prongs. And if this is the sort of stuff that keeps you awake at night, then let me tell you definitively that the dessert spoon should be laid closest to the plate with the bowl of the spoon hollow-side up, pointing to the left and the fork will be laid above it, with the tines pointing to the right. Wherever possible – and sometimes when it's not – you should consume pudding with the fork, because this is the most awkward and ergonomically stupid way to do it.

It's easy enough to make jokes about table-laying or getting laid on a table. It is an innately risible subject, replete with *double entendres* (*entendres* should always be placed on the right with their other meaning facing the person opposite). In fact it is, I think, nearly impossible to write about table setting seriously. The moment you begin to pontificate on the cubic capacity of soup spoons and the advisability of asparagus tongs, you can feel yourself beginning to corpse into helplessly snot-spurting sniggers. But it is, nonetheless, a serious subject. Russian service revolutionised public eating quite as much as piped gas, clean water and democracy. You may look at a table and think, well, what's so complicated about that? I've been eating with a knife and fork since I

was two... and a plate is hardly Pythagorean. But all of it, everything on the table, and its place in relation to everything else, has been considered, worried over and once conceived, invented and refined by someone. We had been eating cooked dinners for 10,000 years before the fork was invented and then it took 20 years to get from Rome to London. It's simple because everyone does it and we don't know the name of the man or the woman who invented it. But that doesn't make Russian service and all the kit and cutlery that goes on a table any less important. It has been as vital to our well-being, culture and politics as offset-litho printing, antisepsis and a codified system of weights and measures. Next time you walk into Zédel, take a moment to look at the tables and wonder at the centuries of trial and ingenuity, the ergonomics of culture, the niceties of hospitality that are implicit in the table setting. It is a work of effortless complexity. And, like all brilliant things, it seems absurd and you can't imagine a world without it.

When the waiter comes to take your order he is practising a trade, a craft, a calling that has been handed on hurriedly in corridors behind swing doors and in white gloved hands, over post-service bottles of beer for 200 years. There are probably manuals on how to be a waiter, but no one has ever become a waiter by reading them. Waiters train each other in passing with humour and irritation and they hand on, for not much money, one of the great pleasures and glories of civilisation.

The 1870s were the birth of the Grand Café; the combination of ideals of an urban working class and the belief in equality and social justice. The Franco-Prussian war ended with the Treaty of Frankfurt which ceded Alsace-Lorraine to Germany. Paris had a sudden influx of refugees from across the new border and many of them, like all refugees, opened cafés. The classic Grand Café menu with its sauerkraut and foie gras shows the heritage of the food from the German border; flavours and ingredients that have travelled across Europe from the Danube and the Black Sea. During the siege Paris starved. First they ate the zoo, serving elephant consommé, kangaroo stew and bear's ribs... and then they ate the cats, dogs and rats. Here was a café menu from 1871.

Consommé de cheval au millet
Brochettes de foie de chien à la maître d'hôtel
Emincé de rable de chat sauce mayonnaise
Epaules et filets de chien braisés. Sauce aux tomates
Civet de chat aux champignons
Salamis de rat sauce Robert
Gigots de chien flanqués de ratons sauce poivrade
Begonias au jus

There is so much there that is utterly French. In the agony of a city starving to death, competing for vermin to eat, still this menu has a panache that is what we have come to expect of the French. It isn't just desperate nutrition but a declaration of hopeless, laughable defiance – saddle of cat comes with mayonnaise. A chef will turn effort into his craft by making a sausage out of rats and then serving it with sauce Robert. Sauce Robert could be a call of clarion national pride to any famished gourmand. It comes from one of the six great French sauces, the mother sauces of French cuisine. It is mentioned by Carème, recorded by François Pierre de la Varenne in the creation tome of French cuisine. It is a variation on *sauce Espagnole* – onions are stewed in butter without colour then combined with a reduction of white wine and pepper with a demi-glace, itself reduced and then finished with mustard. If you don't have a rat, it's also particularly good with pork. The idea that there would be veal bones and off-cuts of beef to make a demi-glace, that they could call up a pound or two of sweet butter, open a bottle of white wine for cooking, is a phantom of liberty; a fundamentalist's belief that culture must transcend the constraints of politics, war – even starvation.

This menu is also an example of something that was central to the idea of the Grand Café Brasserie – no ingredient is too humble, no customer too poor or insignificant not to deserve the finest and most elegant service. When Jeremy and Chris were doing their Stanislavski thing through Zédel's creation they were also aware of the existing grand nineteenth- and early twentieth-century Parisian brasseries like Chartier in the 9th arrondissement.

I returned to Paris as an art student in the 1970s. We would catch the night train from Victoria that arrived at the Gare du Nord in the early morning. We would go to Les Halles and drink onion soup with Cognac and then go to galleries. I particularly remember travelling to see Francis Bacon's greatest exhibition, then we would sleep on floors, get drunk in dozens of cafés on the Left Bank, and inevitably end up somewhere like

Bouillon Chartier for dinner because it was so cheap. Really cheap. And great. You would start with celeriac rémoulade or half a dozen snails, some pâté, main course would be *tête de veau*, *tripe à la mode*, a spoonful or two of daube, trimmed cutlets, a piece of Camembert, a little strawberry tart and a small jug of coarse wine. It was always packed. You pushed in and hovered with discreet menace beside a table that looked like they were finishing. The waiters in their black waistcoats and long white aprons ploughed through the milieu like tugs in a bay of pedalos; they were famous for their efficiency and their terse rudeness. Your order was written on the paper tablecloth and delivered like coal, but all this took place in a room of amazing beauty with fantastic murals, *fin-de-siècle* ironwork, elaborate coat racks and sideboards. The furniture was basic and worn, the customers mostly students, backpackers, street workers and the unlucky, but the room was a palace. At the time Paris had a strict policy of *prix-fixe*

menus. Every restaurant had to offer a cheap menu on its *carte* – depending on their grandeur it could be for as little as nine francs, but it meant that the rich subsidised the food of the poor without charity, without humiliation, so that everyone could afford to eat out.

Gastronomy is an integral part of culture and a civilised life. Paris believed that everybody had a right to take part in it; not just a right but the obligation to understand and know the aesthetic textures and flavours, the smells and the craft of their nation. Everybody was invited to dinner. To eat France. So the street sweeper in his blue overalls would be as critical and knowledgeable about the quality of his beef as the mayor. He would sniff his wine with the same finickity long-nose nous. The *prix-fixe* menu was possibly the most civilised and humane ordinance ever passed by a democratic government. A simple manager of social mobility and homogeneity that cost virtually nothing, needed no capital outlay, infrastructure, no bureaucracy with minimal policing. It was, incidentally, practised briefly in London; during the war and rationing no restaurant could charge more than five shillings for lunch, so you could eat at the Dorchester or the Ritz for a couple of half crowns. You didn't get much and they charged you a lot extra for the cover charge and a drink and of course the food was still English, but for a moment everybody got to sit at the top table. It is telling that the English had to be literally bombed into relaxing their clubbable, exclusive class system.

Zédel has taken the *prix-fixe* model of the grand Parisian brasserie and brought it back to London without a shot being fired. Its set menu is always not just affordable, but cheap. Cheap doesn't mean undistinguished. The three courses are classic French brasserie dishes. You can also eat for a lot more, though this is by no means an expensive restaurant by West End standards. The *prix-fixe* box permanently displayed is a sign, an indicator, it sets a tone. Jeremy and Chris are very fond of indicators, semi-submerged signals and winking permissions in a menu. They will tell you that this is not just a list of food and its cost, it is a coded series of aspirations, assumptions and permissions. We are all so used to reading menus that we don't even notice their subtext but they can tell you how you might behave, what to wear, the other people you're likely to see here, the aspirations of the kitchen, the haughtiness of the staff, the general class of the meal you will be offered and the sort of evening you can expect to have. A menu can even predict your conversation. The *prix-fixe* menu tells you that this is a restaurant for everyone, that all are welcome. This is exclusive only in that it will naturally exclude those who need expense and snobbery to support their social insecurity.

Zédel was started in a grand tradition of brasseries for the wealth of all Londoners – be they long-term or transient. It will give them a room that is as grand as any gentleman's club or expense-account hotel, because the lunch of the common man is as important to the well-being of the city and the state as the plutocrat's business lunch and the wafting ladies with their shopping bags who lunch. And if you say, 'Isn't this all a bit dialectic? A bit George Orwell Champagne Socialism? After all, it's just chopped carrot'. Then you misunderstand the importance of carrot. And that this is not about everybody being the same, or eating the same; it's not a *Les Misérables* call for a national cafeteria of uniform grey food, but a belief that we should all be able to eat off the same menu and that that menu should reflect the diversity of the population. If you sit in the restaurant at lunchtime you will notice a greater variety of people than you would normally expect to find in a West End dining room. There will be journalists here, people from the local film business, actors rehearsing for West End shows and their agents, there will be shop assistants from

Regent Street and Piccadilly, tourists brought in by internet guides, there will be trippers down from the further reaches of Britain come for a weekend to see a show and visit their kids sharing dovecote digs. There will be immigrants to the city – the new Londoners. And there will be the loafers and the wanderers. It is always an engaging and inclusive egalitarian collection that is greater than the sum of its disparate parts.

London's restaurants have grown ever more exclusive and expensive, relying on a broad band of very rich customers in the financial sector and those other economic immigrants, the ones who are refugees because they have too much money rather than too little. It means that the people who service the city, who wait at its tables, deliver its goods, pace its shops, can't afford to take part in the gastronomic life of this city. London is particularly bad at leaving the medium and cheap range of dining to generic chain. So the gastronomic renaissance that we hear so much about is only second hand for most workers in London. They can read about it in magazines, their book shops are stuffed with the recipes of a new and enlightened, ethical, culturally sensitive, healthy and delicious food... they just can't afford to eat it.

Zédel's ethos is unashamedly nostalgic. It isn't part of a contemporary gastro-social movement, it looks back to something that is being lost. A type of French cooking and eating that has grown rare even in France – the local cafés of Paris are as powerless and endangered as the local pubs of London.

The *prix-fixe* menu as I write is *carottes rapées*, *steak haché* and *tarte aux fruits*. *Carottes rapées* is one of the most unexpected French dishes but also one of its most typical. It cuts against every English prejudice about French food whilst being a perfect example of all its virtues. It is just grated carrot with a light dressing. It is ubiquitous across France – in cafés, bistros, restaurants. You can buy it ready bagged in supermarkets. The French really can't eat

enough grated carrot and I can't think of another country that would consider it a stand-alone course at all. In vegetarian cafeterias you may find grated carrot mixed with raisins and pine nuts and a tahini dressing that diminishes and humiliates each ingredient. If you've never bothered trying *carottes rapées* because you imagine it's the cheap option – or worse, the slimmer's option (nothing in classic French food is made with a view to weight loss) – then you must try it. It will be, if not a revelation, then at least a pleasant surprise. The carrot is so familiar, so utilitarianly five-a-day virtuous, such a side-of-the-plate banality that by the simple act of hand grating it into strips slightly thinner than a matchstick it is transformed. Orange root becomes spectacular – freed from the overwhelming crunch of its texture it becomes light and elegantly limpid. So you realise, perhaps for the first time, what a delicate and delicious flavour the carrot has; sweet and fresh and aromatic. A Cinderella vegetable transformed in the kitchen to be the star of a banquet. A carrot you realise is not like anything else – it is just like a carrot. Other things may imitate carrots, but it is solely and only itself. It isn't even remotely like its close relatives – parsley, fennel, dill and cumin. The modern carrot originated in Afghanistan (why, you ask, didn't they just stick with that and say no to the heroin?). It arrived in Europe, like so much of our table, via the Moors through Spain and was being grown in England by the sixteenth century. Selective husbandry made it sweeter and reduced the woodiness of its core. There is a persistent, possibly apocryphal story that the Dutch bred the orange carrot along with the black tulip in a fit of vegetable nationalism – orange being the colour of their football team and their royal family who took the name House of Orange as a bit of early royal branding. But I think, and I'm not alone in this, that it's just as likely that the Dutch chose their national colour having eaten *carottes rapées* and been transfixed by its loveliness.

I feel sure that the king wanted to call himself 'Carrot I' from the House of Carrot – but was dissuaded.

The *carottes rapées* isn't just a surprisingly good starter for the price of a bus fare, it is also a parable. If you think that dinner is just roots and muscle and that anything more airy-fairy is pretentious bilge, then you really don't know what you're putting in your mouth. The *carottes rapées* is the illustration of the purpose of the *prix-fixe* menu. It is that little sign, that wink of permission. It takes a cheap, over-looked ingredient, something that is used in the mélange of soup and stock and stew, one of the great unwashed of the kitchen delivered by the sack, used as bulk and bland background; the anonymous earth-bound workers of cuisine. This dish takes it and raises it with consideration and care and thought to be the best it can. To transcend its humble origins, its immigrant status, to confound those who believe in gastronomic eugenics, who think that grandeur and sophistication are the property of only higher annals

– muscle and blood – and you realise that the carrot was never merely humble; it was always extraordinary and elegant and gamine and amusing. That it was just snobbery and prejudice that kept it in the vegetable box, the stockpot and hidden in the Bolognese, and you might realise all of a sudden that you've been a bit of a carrot most of your life – and this is the point of French food. It is the edible illustration of a transformed, cultured and fair society. It is the distinction between their belief in liberty and the Anglo-Saxon tradition of freedom – which may sound like synonyms, but are different in a fundamental detail. You are born free, but you are given your liberty. Liberty in France is the gift of the state to its citizens. It is managed and directed and it comes with rules. Freedom you exchange or compromise for rules and restrictions for the sake of order and fairness. Freedom comes from the bottom up, liberty from the top down. The Grand Café is an example of delegated liberty, the pub

of licensed freedom. Kitchens work best when given their liberty. You should be careful not to become obsessively fond of *carottes rapées* – overindulgence can lead to a benign condition (carotenosis) where the skin turns orange. Also known as Essex-ism.

The main course on our *prix-fixe* menu is *steak haché*, which is generally translated as beef burger. Indeed the French often call it *le beef burger* and though the two have essentially identical recipes, they are twins separated at birth with very different stories. The hamburger is classed as the sandwich. Classic French cuisine regards the sandwich as the work of supreme philistinism or 'English' – which amounts to the same thing. Sandwiches deny all the founding beliefs and principles of the French table, which dictates that food should be eaten sitting down at a table designated for the purpose – not a desk, not a sofa, not a park bench. Lunch should take at least an hour and preferably two. And a meal that can be consumed in five minutes is medicine and probably the wrong sort of medicine. As a French chef once told me categorically: 'A sandwich is a suppository taken the wrong way'. The hamburger was born out of the brand new twentieth century and the need to eat on the move – it is the invention of the freeway, the pit-stop and the diner. It is gas for humans. And the French enjoy it in an ironic way, always ordering it with a fake American accent or making some droll reference to Clint Eastwood who they think is a Yankee Jean-Paul Sartre. *Le steak haché*, altogether essentially identical to the burger, comes without a bun. This is an important distinction. Not having a bun excuses it from being a sandwich and therefore tasteless. It is topless, like French women on Mediterranean beaches: oiled and brown on the outside, warm and pink on the inside. *Le steak haché* was created in France in the 1960s as food for national service conscripts.

Roland Barthes, the French philosopher and semiotician, who was never photographed without an existentialist snout and a look of supreme Gallic self-satisfaction, pointed out or perhaps uncovered in his book *Mythologies*, that beef, like red wine, was a sanguinary leitmotif for the bourgeoisie. The stuff of Frenchness. The blood of the meat represented the life-blood of the motherland. The French saw in beef the simplicity and complexity of their nation – its culinary generosity, its domestic healthfulness and Epicurean sophistication. *Le bœuf steak* was an emblem of the national character – it can be cheap and toughly-tasty in a modest workers café, or expensively coutured in an haute-cuisine dining room. Steak was, he said, what Frenchmen dreamt of abroad, only slightly hindered by the fact that Americans also seem to dream of it and claimed steak as their national symbol, too.

RECIPES

CAROTTES RAPEES ☞ *serves 4*

- 400g large carrots, peeled and grated
- 120g banana shallots, finely chopped
- pinch of salt
- pinch of ground white pepper
- 100ml Vinaigrette Maison (see page 86)
- 1 tablespoon chopped curly-leaf parsley

Put the carrots, shallots, salt, white pepper and 80ml of the Vinaigrette Maison in a mixing bowl and mix together until the vinaigrette binds the ingredients together.

Using 2 tablespoons, squeeze as much mixture as you can between the spoons and turn the spoons tightly to create a quenelle shape (a 3-sided oval). Place one in the middle of each serving plate, then sprinkle the parsley over the top and dress with a touch more vinaigrette.

CELERI REMOULADE ☞ *serves 4*

- 1 celeriac, peeled
- ½ lemon
- 200ml mayonnaise
- 100g Dijon mustard
- 1 tablespoon chopped flat-leaf parsley
- 50ml extra virgin olive oil
- salt and ground black pepper

Using a kitchen mandolin or a box grater, shred the celeriac as thick as a matchstick and squeeze over the juice from the half lemon. In a separate bowl, mix together the mayonnaise, mustard and most of the parsley (reserving some to garnish). Season to taste.

Add the shredded celeriac to the mayonnaise mixture and gently mix. Using 2 tablespoons, squeeze as much mixture as you can between the spoons and turn the spoons tightly to create a quenelle shape (a 3-sided oval). Place one in the middle of each serving plate, garnish with parsley and dress with a touch of extra virgin olive oil.

SOUPE A L'OIGNON

50g butter

50ml olive oil

2 large or 4 small onions, sliced

2 garlic cloves, finely sliced

1 teaspoon caster sugar

1 tablespoon plain flour

200ml dry white wine

1.5 litres beef stock (stock cubes are fine)

1 bay leaf and 8 sprigs of thyme, tied together with string

4–8 slices of French bread

140g Gruyère, grated

salt and ground black pepper

Melt the butter with the oil in a heavy-based pan, then add the onions and garlic. Cover and cook over a low heat for around 10 minutes until soft, then stir in the sugar. Cook over a medium heat, uncovered, for a further 10 minutes, stirring frequently, until the onions are starting to become caramelised, being careful not to burn them.

Stir in the flour, followed by the wine. Reduce the wine slightly, then add the stock and herb bundle. Cover and cook over a low heat for a minimum of 20 minutes. Season well.

Meanwhile, to make the croûtons, toast the bread slices, then divide the grated cheese between them and melt under the grill. Divide the hot soup between 4 bowls and float the croûtons on top.

NOTE

You can use tinned beef consommé in place of the beef stock.

ŒUFS DURS MAYONNAISE

8 medium eggs

1 iceberg lettuce, washed and shredded

100ml mayonnaise

30ml Vinaigrette Maison (see page 86)

1 tablespoon chopped chives

sea salt and Espelette pepper

Cook the eggs in their shells for 5 minutes, leave to cool then peel. Take 2 of the eggs and separate the yolk from the white, then grate the yolks and whites separately. Cut the remaining 6 eggs in half.

Dress the shredded iceberg with the Vinaigrette Maison. Place a handful of the iceberg in the centre of each serving plate. Place 3 small drops of mayonnaise around the iceberg, then place an egg half on each drop of mayonnaise. Sprinkle the grated egg yolk and white separately over the iceberg.

Spoon (or pipe) the remaining mayonnaise on top of the eggs and sprinkle the chives evenly on top. Finish with a pinch of salt and a light dusting of Espelette pepper.

NOTE

Espelette is a finely ground chilli pepper from the town by the same name in southwest France.

SALADE D'ENDIVES AU ROQUEFORT

serves 4

3 heads of white chicory

100ml Vinaigrette Maison (see page 86)

1 teaspoon chopped chives

80g Roquefort, crumbled

60g toasted walnuts

Separate out the chicory leaves and place in a bowl with the Vinaigrette Maison and chives.

Divide the leaves between 4 plates, stacking them across each other (see photograph opposite).

Place the walnuts in and around the leaves and crumble the Roquefort pieces on top. Drizzle with any leftover vinaigrette from the bowl.

PATE DE CAMPAGNE

- 2 rabbit legs, meat cleaned off the bone and finely chopped
- 2 pigeon breasts, skin removed, finely chopped
- 250g chicken liver, finely chopped
- 275g pork fat, minced
- 200g unsalted pork belly, minced
- 400g pork shoulder, minced
- 2 small shallots, chopped
- 2 garlic cloves, finely chopped
- 50ml French brandy
- 80ml white wine
- 1 level teaspoon ground white pepper
- 1 level teaspoon table salt
- 1 level teaspoon ground quatre épices
- 12 slices of unsmoked rindless streaky bacon
- 5 bay leaves
- 5 sprigs of thyme

Place all the ingredients except the bacon, bay and thyme in a large bowl and mix together thoroughly. Cover and leave in the fridge to marinate for 24 hours.

Preheat the oven to 160°C/320°F/Gas 3. Line a 1.7-litre terrine mould, 34 x 12cm and 11cm deep, with a double layer of cling film. Use the bacon to line the mould inside the cling film, bashing it out slightly if necessary, so that it is long enough to over-hang the sides.

Fill the mould with the pâté mixture and bring the over-hanging bacon back over to cover. Arrange the bay leaves and thyme on top and cover the mould with a double layer of foil so it just covers the lip. Half-fill a baking tray with hot water, place the terrine in the tray and bake for 90 minutes (the terrine needs to reach a minimum of 75°C). Once cooked, leave to cool completely before removing from the mould and on to a clean tray. You may want to place weights on top to compact the terrine together. Serve with crusty bread and pickles.

SIX ESCARGOTS AU BEURRE PERSILLÉ

serves 4

250g unsalted butter, at room temperature

150g garlic purée (available in supermarkets)

12 large stalks of curly-leaf parsley, leaves picked and very finely chopped

60ml Pernod or Ricard (optional)

24 cooked snails (from a supermarket, deli or fishmonger, or cook your own)

handful of breadcrumbs

salt and ground black pepper

Preheat the oven to 190°C/375°F/Gas 5 and the grill to high.

Soften the butter in a mixing bowl, then add the garlic purée and parsley and mix well. Season to taste and fold in the alcohol, if using.

Place the snails in a snail dish, divide the flavoured butter evenly between them and sprinkle the breadcrumbs over the top.

Bake in the oven for 4 minutes then flash under the hot grill.

NOTE

You can make your beurre persillé in advance, roll in cling film in a sausage shape and refrigerate until required.

TARTARE DE SAUMON

200g fresh salmon, finely diced

200g smoked salmon trimmings
(ask your fishmonger for these)

100g shallots, finely chopped

5 sprigs of dill, finely chopped,
plus an extra sprig to serve

30ml olive oil, plus extra for drizzling

generous pinch of table salt

1 teaspoon ground white pepper

finely grated zest and juice of 1 lemon

1 tablespoon crème fraîche

4 teaspoons salmon caviar (from a small jar)

4 sprigs of chervil

1 cucumber, halved lengthways, deseeded,
peeled and thinly sliced

Espelette pepper (see Note on page 42)

Put the fresh and smoked salmon, shallots, dill, olive oil, salt, pepper and lemon zest in a mixing bowl. Mix well until combined.

Divide the mixture evenly between 4 plates. Using 2 teaspoons, take a little crème fraîche between the spoons and turn the spoons tightly to create a quenelle shape (a 3-sided oval). Place a quenelle on top of each serving of salmon, and top with a teaspoon of salmon caviar and a chervil sprig.

Arrange the cucumber slices around the salmon, drizzle a little olive oil around the plate and sprinkle a touch of Espelette over the plate. Tear up the extra sprig of dill and scatter over each plate.

Just before serving, carefully spoon a little lemon juice onto each portion.

TARTE AUX POIREAUX ET GRUYERE

☞ *serves 8*

3 leeks, white parts only, washed and sliced

1 onion, diced

30ml olive oil

500g shortcrust pastry (or buy a pre-cooked tart case)

50ml double cream

50ml milk

2 large eggs

pinch of sea salt

pinch of ground white pepper

100g Gruyère, grated

20g lamb's lettuce

Gently sweat the leeks and onion in the olive oil until translucent, then set aside to cool. Preheat the oven to 150°C/300°F/Gas 3.

Roll out the pastry to fit a 30cm-diameter tart tin, then blind bake for 20 minutes (see Tarte au Citron on page 88).

In a large jug, mix together the cream, milk, eggs, salt and pepper. Stir in the cooled leek and onion mixture and half of the Gruyère. Pour into the pastry case, spread out the mixture then sprinkle the remaining Gruyère evenly over the top.

Cook in the oven for 35 minutes, or until the filling looks golden. Leave to cool for 30 minutes before cutting into wedges and serving with the lamb's lettuce.

BRANDADE DE MORUE

600g cod fillet

5 garlic cloves, peeled and slightly crushed

2 tablespoons sea salt

4 sprigs of thyme

6 sprigs of flat-leaf parsley, leaves finely chopped and stalks reserved

350ml olive oil

200ml whole milk

300g freshly boiled and mashed Maris Piper potatoes

1 lemon

salt and ground black pepper

Place the cod in a pan with the garlic, salt, thyme, parsley stalks, 50ml of the olive oil and all the milk. Cover and simmer for 10 minutes until the cod flakes. Strain the liquid into a jug or bowl and place the cooked fish in a mixing bowl. Discard the thyme sprigs and parsley stalks, pick out the garlic cloves, which should be soft, then pound to a paste and add to the fish.

Put the fish mixture and mashed potatoes in a dish, pour in 200ml of the olive oil and fold together. Season to taste.

Scoop the warm brandade onto 4 plates and finely zest the lemon over the top of each. Sprinkle over the chopped parsley, drizzle with the remaining olive oil and serve.

NOTE

Brandade should be quite salty, with a silky texture from the addition of the olive oil.

TRUITE AUX AMANDES

4 rainbow trout, gutted and scaled (ask your fishmonger to do this)

plain flour, for dusting

about 200ml vegetable oil

140g unsalted butter

juice of 2 lemons

small handful of curly-leaf parsley, chopped

1 tablespoon small capers

20g toasted flaked almonds

sea salt and ground black pepper

Season the trout inside and out and lightly dust with flour. Add enough oil to a non-stick frying pan to cover the base, and heat. When hot, carefully place the fish in the pan, in 2 batches if necessary. Lightly shake the pan after 30 seconds to ensure the fish doesn't stick to the base. Fry for 4 minutes, then turn the fish over using a palette knife or fish slice and cook for a further 4 minutes.

Test the fish is cooked by sliding a knife into the backbone area. Leave for 15 seconds then remove; the knife should be hot. Remove the fish and keep warm, then pour away the excess oil, place the pan back on the heat and add the butter. Heat until it starts to look nutty brown, then pour in the lemon juice. When the butter froths up, throw in the parsley and capers.

Transfer the fish to 4 plates, spoon the parsley and caper butter evenly over each fish and sprinkle with the flaked almonds. Serve with vegetables of your choice.

VOL-AU-VENT AUX FRUITS DE MER

25g unsalted butter

1 shallot, finely chopped

1 garlic clove, finely chopped

100g button mushrooms, sliced

1 tablespoon tomato purée

200ml white wine

500g frozen seafood mix (follow packet instructions on defrosting and blanch in boiling water before adding)

50ml double cream

small bunch of dill, chopped, plus extra to serve

4 x 10-cm puff pastry cases (ready-made, or home-made using bought puff pastry)

FOR THE VELOUTE

50g unsalted butter

50g plain flour

500ml hot fish stock (stock cubes are fine)

salt and ground black pepper

For the velouté, melt the butter in a heavy-based pan, add the flour and cook over a moderate heat for 4–5 minutes, stirring all the time with a wooden spoon. Gradually add the hot fish stock, in small amounts, until you have used it all and the sauce is smooth and slightly thick. Leave to cook over a low heat until you can no longer taste the flour, then season and remove from the heat.

Melt the 25g butter in another pan, add the shallot and garlic and sauté without letting them colour. Add the mushrooms and cook for 3 minutes. Add the tomato purée and wine and cook until the wine has evaporated. Add the velouté and bring to the boil, then add the seafood and cook gently until piping hot. Add the cream and dill and season to taste.

Warm the vol-au-vent cases in a medium-hot oven, place on plates and divide the seafood mixture between them. Finish with the extra dill.

MOULES MARINIERES

800g fresh mussels, scrubbed and washed (you can ask your fishmonger to do this)

1 small onion, finely chopped

2 garlic cloves, finely chopped

200ml white wine

200ml double cream

1 tablespoon chopped flat-leaf parsley

Heat a large heavy-based pan, tip in the mussels and place the lid on for 30 seconds. Remove the lid and add the onion, garlic and wine. Put the lid back on immediately and shake the pot. The heat from the liquid will steam the mussels open.

After 4 minutes, remove the lid (you should see the shells splitting open, a sign that they are almost cooked), pour in the cream and replace the lid for a further 2 minutes.

Put the mussels, which should be fully opened, in 4 bowls, sprinkle over the parsley and serve with some crusty French bread.

ROUGET A LA NICOISE

80g green beans

80g new potatoes, peeled

80g black olives, pitted and halved

1 banana shallot, sliced

100g slow-roasted or sun-dried tomatoes,
cut in half if large

100ml Vinaigrette Maison (see page 86)

50ml olive oil

4 large red mullet fillets (ask your fishmonger
to remove the pin bones)

8 tinned anchovy fillets in oil, drained

200ml mayonnaise (with an optional squeeze
of lemon juice)

sea salt and ground black pepper

NOTE

To slow-roast your own tomatoes, place
tomato halves cut side up on a baking tray,
season and cook in a low oven for 90 minutes.

Niçoise usually includes eggs, but here the
egg component is in the added mayonnaise.

Cook the beans and potatoes in separate saucepans
of boiling water until tender, then drain. Allow to
cool slightly, then cut the potatoes into chunks and
halve the beans, if long.

Put the beans, potatoes, olives, shallot, tomatoes
and Vinaigrette Maison in a bowl. Add a pinch each
of salt and pepper, mix gently and arrange on 4 plates.

Heat the olive oil in a non-stick frying pan.
Season the red mullet and place, skin side down, in
the hot pan. Press firmly on the fish with a spatula
to prevent the fillet from curling. Cook for 2 minutes,
then carefully turn the fish over and cook for a
further 2 minutes. Remove from the pan and place
a fillet on each plate, over the salad.

Place an anchovy and a spoonful of mayonnaise
on each plate.

STEAK HACHÉ, SAUCE AU POIVRE

FOR THE HACHE

800g chuck steak mince (ask your butcher to mince it for you)

1 large egg

1 teaspoon English mustard (or Dijon if you prefer)

1 teaspoon tomato ketchup

a little oil, for rubbing

salt and ground black pepper

FOR THE PEPPERCORN SAUCE

50ml rapeseed oil

2 tablespoons cracked black pepper

100ml brandy

200ml beef stock (stock cubes are fine)

500ml double cream

1 tablespoon chopped curly-leaf parsley

1 tablespoon green peppercorns

For the haché, mix the steak mince, egg, mustard and ketchup together and season lightly. To check the seasoning, break off a touch and fry, then taste and adjust as necessary. Divide the remaining meat into 4 and shape into patties. Leave to chill in the fridge.

For the peppercorn sauce, heat up a heavy-based saucepan, add the oil, then the cracked black pepper, stir briefly then turn down the heat and carefully add the brandy. Once the brandy has reduced, add the stock, reduce down until slightly thick, then add the cream. Stir and leave to simmer until the flavour and consistency are as you want them, then turn down to low and leave while you cook the hachés.

Rub each haché with a touch of oil, and season. Heat up a hot griddle pan or non-stick frying pan, add the hachés and cook for 6 minutes on each side. Serve with the peppercorn sauce, your favourite type of frites – chunky, thin, curly (the crunchier the better for this dish) – and the chopped parsley and green peppercorns.

LAPIN A LA MOUTARDE

1 whole rabbit, cut into 8 pieces (ask your butcher to divide into 2 legs, 2 shoulders and 4 pieces from the saddle)

Dijon mustard, for coating

50g butter

50ml rapeseed oil

1 large banana shallot, diced

2 garlic cloves, sliced

1 bay leaf

3 sprigs of rosemary

300ml dry white wine

1 litre chicken stock (stock cubes are fine)

600ml double cream

1 tablespoon grainy mustard

salt and ground black pepper

Season the rabbit then rub the pieces all over with Dijon mustard. (Cook straightaway, or cover and refrigerate to marinate for up to 24 hours.) Heat the butter and oil in a heavy-based pan, add the rabbit pieces, fry until golden-brown then remove to a plate. Add the shallot, garlic, bay leaf and rosemary to the pan and cook, stirring, for 4–5 minutes, ensuring the garlic doesn't colour. Add the wine and reduce until almost evaporated.

Add the stock and return the rabbit pieces to the pan. Cook, uncovered, until the stock has reduced by three quarters, then add the cream. Bring to the boil and simmer, uncovered, until the rabbit is tender and the sauce coats the rabbit – you may have to add a touch more stock a little at a time if it becomes thick and the rabbit is still firm. Stir in the grainy mustard, season to taste and serve with pasta, sauté potatoes or plain rice.

BŒUF BOURGUIGNON

- 1kg feather blade beef steak, cut into chunks
- 750ml bottle of red wine (preferably Burgundy)
- plain flour, for dusting
- 150ml rapeseed oil
- 100g smoked streaky bacon, finely diced
- 3 garlic cloves, sliced
- 200g pearl onions or small shallots, peeled and left whole
- 200g chestnut mushrooms, quartered
- 6 sprigs of thyme
- 2 bay leaves
- 1 tablespoon tomato purée
- about 1 litre beef stock (stock cubes are fine)
- sea salt and ground black pepper

Put the beef into a bowl or dish, pour over enough wine to cover (about half the bottle) and set aside to marinate for a few hours. Drain in a colander, reserving the wine.

Pat the beef dry with kitchen paper, season lightly and dust with a touch of flour. Heat about three quarters of the oil in a heavy-based pan, then add the beef and fry until golden-brown on all sides. Remove the beef to a plate and add the rest of the oil to the pan. Fry the bacon for a few minutes, then add the garlic and onions and cook until golden-brown. Add the mushrooms, thyme and bay leaves and cook for a further 2 minutes. Stir in the tomato purée, add back the browned beef and cook for another 3–4 minutes, then pour in the reserved marinade wine and the remaining wine in the bottle.

Cook over a high heat for about 30 minutes, or until the wine has reduced. Then add beef stock to cover the meat, stir and place a lid on top, leaving it slightly ajar. Turn the heat down and simmer for a few hours, occasionally checking the stock levels and adding more if needed. The sauce should get thicker and richer as it cooks. When the beef is tender, season to taste and serve with good mashed potato.

COUSCOUS A L'AGNEAU ET MERGUEZ

180g couscous

50g unsalted butter

grated zest and juice of 1 lemon

1 parsnip, cut into 2-cm cubes

1 carrot, cut into 2-cm cubes

400g tin of chickpeas, drained

400g lamb shoulder, cut into large chunks

8 merguez sausages (see Note below)

100g chamoula sauce or a similar 'hot' sauce (see Note below)

small handful of mint, very finely shredded

NOTE

Merguez sausages can be found in local supermarkets or delis.

Chamoula sauce is a classic, hot, spiced tomato sauce served with Moroccan fish and meat dishes. Ask your local deli for an alternative if they don't stock it.

Put the couscous in a heatproof bowl and pour in enough boiling water to come 2cm above the level of the couscous. Cover the bowl with a plate and set aside for 5–10 minutes or until the couscous grains have swelled and there's no water left.

Melt the butter in a saucepan. Add the lemon zest and juice, followed by the cooked couscous, the vegetables and chickpeas. Heat gently.

Meanwhile, thread the lamb pieces onto metal skewers and grill under a hot grill or on a hot griddle pan alongside the merguez sausages. (Do this in batches if necessary.) Turn frequently to cook evenly, around 6–8 minutes depending on the size of the lamb pieces.

Heat the chamoula sauce in a separate pan.

Once everything is cooked, put the vegetable couscous on 4 plates, top with the chamoula sauce and finish with the lamb and sausages. Sprinkle the mint over the top.

POULET AU CHAMPAGNE

- 125g unsalted butter
- 1 medium chicken, jointed into 8 pieces (you can ask your butcher to do this)
- plain flour, for dusting
- 1 large onion, finely diced
- 3 garlic cloves, sliced
- 100g unsmoked streaky bacon, cut into lardons
- 1 bay leaf
- pinch of dried thyme
- 400ml Champagne
- 1 litre chicken stock (stock cubes are fine)
- 600ml double cream
- salt and ground black pepper

Heat the butter in a heavy-based pan. Lightly season and dust the chicken pieces in flour, place in the pan and fry until golden brown all over. Remove to a plate and add the onion, garlic, bacon, bay and thyme to the pan. Fry, stirring, for about 5 minutes.

Add the Champagne and cook until reduced, then pour in the stock and add the chicken pieces back in. Cook over a moderate heat, uncovered, until the liquid has reduced by a third, then add the cream, stir and cook over a moderate heat for about 15 minutes, until the sauce becomes thick enough to coat the chicken and the chicken is tender. Divide between 4 plates and serve with potatoes or pappardelle.

CHOUCROUTE ALSACIENNE

400g pork belly

8 new potatoes, peeled

4 Frankfurter sausages

4 x 100g pieces of cured smoked belly (this comes pre-cooked)

100g garlic sausage

100g Morteau smoked sausage

1 bay leaf

1 litre chicken stock (stock cubes are fine)

400g sauerkraut

1 small jar (about 200ml) of duck fat

120ml Riesling

small handful of curly-leaf parsley, chopped

Place the pork belly in a pan with just enough cold water to cover, bring to the boil and simmer for about 70 minutes until tender, then drain. When the belly is nearly ready, cook the potatoes in a saucepan of water until tender; drain.

Put the Frankfurters, smoked belly, garlic sausage, smoked sausage, bay leaf and the cooked belly with the stock into a large saucepan and bring to the boil. Add the drained potatoes, then turn down the heat and leave to simmer gently until needed.

Heat the sauerkraut in a separate saucepan, and the duck fat in another small pan.

To serve, spoon the warmed sauerkraut onto plates, cut the pork belly into 4 slices, the garlic sausage into slices and the smoked sausage into thin slices. Arrange all the meats and potatoes on the plates. Finish with a spoonful of melted duck fat, splashes of Riesling and the parsley.

NOTE

Sauerkraut, 'sour cabbage', has a distinctive tart flavour, and when eaten with the salted meat and Riesling you will taste the balance of the flavours.

SALADE VERTE ET RADIS

2 butter leaf lettuces

60ml Vinaigrette Maison (see page 86)

6 breakfast radishes (the long tubular ones), finely sliced

sea salt and ground black pepper

Remove the outside leaves from the lettuces, split the heads in half and carefully break out the core. Break up the leaves, rinse quickly under cold water then shake dry. Place the leaves in a large mixing bowl and add the Vinaigrette Maison. Toss carefully, adding a pinch each of salt and pepper.

Divide the salad leaves between 4 plates or bowls and top with the radish slices.

PETITS POIS
A LA FRANCAISE

30g unsalted butter

1 small onion, diced

300ml warm chicken or vegetable stock (stock cubes are fine)

400g frozen 'petits pois' peas

½ small iceberg lettuce

6 fresh mint leaves

salt and ground black pepper

Melt the butter in a large saucepan, add the onion and sauté gently until soft, without letting it brown. Add the stock and simmer for 3 minutes, then drop in the peas, season generously and simmer for 15 minutes.

Just before the peas are ready, shred the lettuce and mint. Remove the pan from the heat, add the shredded lettuce and mint, give it a stir and serve.

GRATIN DAUPHINOIS

300ml double cream

125ml whole milk

4 garlic cloves, peeled and bashed

4 sprigs of thyme

1 bay leaf

1kg King Edward potatoes, or other floury variety, peeled and thinly sliced

150g Gruyère, grated

salt and ground black pepper

Preheat the oven to 190°C/375°F/Gas 5.

Put the cream, milk, garlic, thyme and bay leaf in a pan and bring to the boil. Remove from the heat and set aside to cool and to allow the garlic and herbs to infuse the cream and milk.

Place the sliced potatoes in a large bowl and pour the cooled cream mixture through a sieve onto the potatoes. Season well and mix thoroughly. Spread the potatoes out evenly in an ovenproof dish (about 24 x 18 x 5cm), pressing carefully but firmly to ensure there are no gaps and the liquid sinks in. Sprinkle the Gruyère evenly over the top.

Cover the dish tightly with foil and transfer to the preheated oven for 30 minutes, then remove the foil and continue to cook for a further 20 minutes. Test with a sharp knife, and if the potatoes are still slightly firm, cook for a further 15 minutes. Any leftovers can be kept for 2 days and reheated.

RATATOUILLE

200ml olive oil

1 large aubergine, cubed

1 small red onion, cubed

3 garlic cloves, finely sliced

1 small yellow pepper, deseeded and cubed

1 small red pepper, deseeded and cubed

1 large courgette, cubed

100ml red wine vinegar

400g tin of chopped tomatoes

small bunch of basil, stalks and leaves separated

salt and ground black pepper

Heat half the oil in a non-stick sauté pan, add the aubergine and cook, stirring, until golden brown. Using a slotted spoon, remove to a plate lined with kitchen paper, to drain.

Heat the remaining oil in the pan and add the onion and garlic. Fry, stirring and without letting them colour, for 5 minutes. Add both peppers and cook for 5 minutes. Add the courgette and cook for a further 5 minutes.

Add the aubergines back to the pan, with the vinegar. Stir and cook for 2–3 minutes, then add the tomatoes with their juice, and the basil stalks. Cook for a further 20 minutes then season to taste.

Just before serving, fold in the basil leaves.

POIS CHICHES A LA TOMATE

☞ serves 4–5

500g dried chickpeas

100ml extra virgin olive oil

2 small garlic cloves, sliced

½ red onion, finely diced

1 small carrot, peeled and finely diced

½ dried chilli, deseeded and chopped

200g tin of cherry tomatoes or chopped tomatoes

½ lemon

½ tablespoon chopped flat-leaf parsley

sea salt and ground black pepper

Soak the chickpeas in plenty of cold water for at least 8 hours, and ideally 24 hours, then drain and transfer to a large saucepan. Cover generously with cold water and simmer gently until soft, about 90 minutes. Drain, reserving the liquor.

Heat the olive oil in a separate pan, add the garlic, onion, carrot and chilli and fry for 5 minutes over a gentle heat, without letting the vegetables colour. Add the tomatoes and cook for 10 minutes, then add the drained chickpeas with a little of the reserved cooking liquor. Cook over a low heat for a further 40 minutes, stirring occasionally.

To finish, finely zest the lemon over the pan, then squeeze in the juice. Add salt and pepper to taste, then stir in the parsley and serve.

VINAIGRETTE MAISON

serves 4

125ml white wine vinegar

1 tablespoon English mustard

1 tablespoon Dijon mustard

1 large banana shallot, finely chopped

375ml extra virgin olive oil

sea salt and ground black pepper

Put the vinegar, both mustards and shallot in a suitably sized bowl, whisk for 2 minutes then slowly whisk in the olive oil. Add salt and pepper to taste. Store in the fridge until required.

NOTE

If the vinaigrette becomes too thick, you can thin it with water.

POMMES DE TERRE

At Zédel, there is a wide variety of potato dishes on the menu throughout the year.

Pommes frites are a strong feature of the menu as we serve these both with our grilled dishes and as a side order. We probably serve more than 50,000kg pommes frites per year. We also serve 'pommes château' (small, barrel shape), 'pommes vapeur' (steamed, peeled new potatoes), 'pommes fondantes' (cylindrical potato cooked in clarified butter), 'pommes purée' (smooth mashed potato), 'pommes Pont Neuf' (stacked potato chips), 'gratin dauphinois' (as seen on page 81).

You will find that recipes for pommes de terre in French cooking usually involve a lot of butter...

TARTE AU CITRON

200g good-quality sweet shortcrust pastry

1 egg yolk, beaten

20g caster sugar per slice, to glaze (optional)

FOR THE FILLING

**juice (120ml) and finely grated zest of
3 lemons**

160g caster sugar

3 medium eggs, lightly beaten

210g cold unsalted butter, cubed

Lightly roll out the pastry to 1cm thick and use to line a 23-cm, 2.5-cm deep, loose-based tart tin. Refrigerate for 20 minutes or freeze for 10 minutes. Preheat the oven to 180°C/350°F/Gas 4.

Line the pastry case with foil and fill with baking beans. Blind bake for 12 minutes, then remove the beans and foil and bake for a further 5–6 minutes, until the pastry is golden-brown all over. Brush the pastry all over with the egg yolk and bake for 2 further minutes (this creates a waterproof seal), then remove from the oven and set aside. Reduce the oven temperature to 140°C/285°F/Gas 1.

Put the lemon juice and sugar in a heatproof mixing bowl. Using an electric hand-held blender (you can use a balloon whisk but it will take longer and the mixture will need to be sieved), gently blend together, then add the eggs and blend further. Place the bowl over a pan of simmering water and add the cubed butter and lemon zest. As the butter starts to melt, whisk the mixture occasionally with a balloon whisk. The mixture will start to thicken after about 4–5 minutes, and it is ready when it coats the back of a spoon and reaches a temperature of around 70°C. Carefully pour into the pastry case, as close to the top of the pastry case as possible.

Bake for 15–20 minutes until set but still with a gentle wobble. Place on a wire rack and leave to cool. Refrigerate for 2–3 hours before serving. If you wish, sprinkle 20g sugar over each slice and caramelise using a cook's blowtorch or under a very hot grill.

CREME BRULEE

☞ *serves 4*

1 vanilla pod, split lengthways

250ml double cream

250ml whipping cream

100ml milk

160g egg yolks (about 8 yolks)

100g caster sugar

60g demerara sugar

NOTE

The method here does not require a bain marie, or water bath, as is usually the case, because the very low oven temperature will set the custard without scrambling the eggs, keeping the custard silky and smooth.

Preheat the oven to 110°C/225°F/Gas ¼.

Scrape the seeds out of the vanilla pod and add both seeds and pod to a pan with both of the creams and the milk. Bring to the boil. In a bowl, whisk together the egg yolks and caster sugar, then add the boiled cream and milk to the yolks and mix well.

Pour the mixture back into the pan and, over a low heat, gently heat to 80°C. (This will ensure the vanilla seeds remain suspended and don't all sink to the bottom of your dish.) Take off the heat and pass through a fine sieve to remove the vanilla pod.

Pour the mixture into four 8–9-cm dishes and bake for 45 minutes or until the custard is set. Use a small knife to check the middle is not still runny; there should be a slight wobble, and as it cools it will firm up. Leave to cool for 20 minutes then refrigerate for at least 3 hours before serving.

When ready to serve, sprinkle the demerara sugar evenly over the tops and caramelise using a cook's blowtorch or under a very hot grill.

TARTE TATIN

200g caster sugar

100g butter, cubed

50ml whipping cream

300g good-quality puff pastry

6 Braeburn apples, peeled, cored and cut in half lengthways

Preheat the oven to 180°C/350°F/Gas 4.

Heat the sugar in a stainless steel saucepan, constantly stirring, until a golden caramel colour. Add the butter and keep stirring until it is incorporated and it has become a nice emulsion. Pour 100g of the caramel into each of two 15-cm non-stick cake tins. Place the remaining caramel in the pan back on the heat and pour in the cream, stirring to create a caramel sauce. Take off the heat and set aside.

Roll out the puff pastry to a thickness of about 3mm, then cut out two 18-cm circles, reserving the trimmings for another use. Arrange the apple halves in a circular pattern, flat-side down, on top of the caramel in the tins, then cover each with a puff pastry disc. Tuck the pastry edges around the apples, inside the tin, to keep the apples tightly packed. Bake in the oven for 30 minutes, then remove from the oven and lightly press on the pastry so the apples will be flattened against the bottom of the tin.

Heat through the reserved caramel sauce, then carefully invert the tins onto a chopping board. Lift off the tins and cut each tart in half. Place a tart half on each serving plate and brush or pour a little of the caramel sauce over them so they look nice and shiny. Serve with vanilla bean ice cream.

RIZ GRAND-MERE

FOR THE CHERRY COMPOTE

150g frozen sour cherries (see Note below)

50g caster sugar

FOR THE RICE PUDDING

400ml whole milk

30g caster sugar

1 vanilla pod, halved lengthways and seeds scraped OR ½ teaspoon grated nutmeg

100g pudding rice

20g salted butter

75g condensed milk

demerara sugar, for sprinkling

For the cherry compote, put the cherries and sugar in a small pan and place over a low heat. Once the cherries have defrosted, turn the heat up and boil slowly for a few minutes to thicken, then remove from the heat and set aside.

For the rice pudding, bring the milk, sugar and vanilla seeds or nutmeg to the boil in a pan. When it reaches the boil, stir in the rice and bring back to the boil. Cook slowly over a gentle heat for about 30 minutes, until the rice is tender, stirring occasionally to prevent it from sticking to the bottom of the pan. Stir in the butter and condensed milk, adjusting the consistency with a little extra milk, if necessary.

To serve, heat up the cherry compote, pour the rice pudding into 4 bowls, spoon the compote on top and sprinkle with demerara sugar.

NOTE

In place of frozen cherries, you can use a fruit compote, diluted with a little water, skipping the first step of the recipe.

ILE FLOTTANTE

oil, for greasing

1 vanilla pod, split lengthways

120g egg whites (4 whites)

squeeze of lemon juice

110g caster sugar

8g egg white powder

100ml milk

caramel and pink praline, to serve

FOR THE VANILLA ANGLAISE

1 vanilla pod

300g double cream

300g milk

120g egg yolks (about 6 yolks)

60g caster sugar

For the vanilla anglaise, scrape the seeds out of the vanilla pod and add both seeds and pod to a pan with the cream and milk. Bring to the boil. In a bowl, whisk together the egg yolks and caster sugar, then pour a third of the boiled cream mixture onto the yolks and mix well. Pour back into the pan and, over a low heat, stir with a wooden spoon, until slightly thickened. Remove from the heat and discard the vanilla pod. Leave to cool before refrigerating.

Preheat the oven to 110°C/225°F/Gas ¼. Grease the insides of four 7.5-cm (and 4-cm deep) stainless steel mousse rings, and the base of a roasting tray. Put the rings in the tray and place a second tray of hot water in the bottom of the oven (to create steam).

Scrape the vanilla seeds into the egg whites in a bowl and add the lemon juice. In a second bowl, whisk the sugar and egg white powder, then add to the egg whites. Using electric beaters, whisk to firm peaks. Transfer to a piping bag and pipe into the metal rings, filling them nearly to the top. Pour the milk into the roasting tray; it should be 5mm deep. Cover with foil and bake for 8–10 minutes. Remove from the oven, take off the foil and cool in the tray. Put the meringues on plates, pour the vanilla anglaise around and drizzle caramel and pink praline on top.

MOUSSE AU CHOCOLAT

100g dark chocolate (70% cocoa solids)

65g caster sugar

75g egg yolks (about 4 yolks)

190g egg whites (about 6 whites)

grated or shaved chocolate, to garnish

Melt the chocolate in a bain marie (or in a heatproof bowl set over a pan of simmering water, making sure the base of the bowl does not touch the water) and keep warm. Meanwhile, whisk 25g of the sugar with the egg yolks in a bowl, until light in colour and foamy. Fold into the warm chocolate and keep warm.

In a clean bowl, whisk the remaining 40g sugar with the egg whites to form soft peaks. Fold a third of the meringue into the chocolate mixture and, when incorporated, fold in the rest, taking care not to lose too much air. Carefully transfer the mousse to a serving bowl and leave to set in the fridge for at least 1 hour. Just before serving, garnish with chocolate and scoop into bowls at the table.

BAVAROIS VANILLE ET FRAMBOISE

serves 4

FOR THE RASPBERRY JELLY

1 gelatine leaf (about 3g)

100g raspberry purée

20g caster sugar

8 fresh raspberries, plus 4 extra to serve

FOR THE BAVAROIS

1½ gelatine leaves

230g crème fraîche

20g dark rum

300ml double cream

45g caster sugar

1 vanilla pod, halved lengthways and seeds scraped

4 fresh raspberries, to serve

For the raspberry jelly, place the gelatine leaf in a small bowl of cold water for 5 minutes, to hydrate. Meanwhile, place the raspberry purée and sugar in a small pan and heat until hot. Drain the gelatine, squeeze to remove excess water, then add to the hot purée and stir to dissolve.

Place 2 fresh raspberries in the bottom of each of 4 martini glasses, pour the raspberry jelly evenly into each glass and put to one side to set.

For the bavarois, place the gelatine leaves in a small bowl of cold water. Stir the crème fraîche and rum together in a heatproof bowl and set aside. Bring the double cream, sugar and vanilla seeds to the boil in a pan, then take off the heat. Drain the gelatine, squeezing out any excess water, and add to the cream and sugar mixture, stirring to dissolve. Pour this mixture over the crème fraîche and rum mixture and stir with a balloon whisk until smooth. Let the mixture cool completely until it just starts to set but is still pourable. Pour the bavarois mixture over the set jelly up to the rim of each glass and refrigerate for at least 3 hours. To serve, garnish with a fresh raspberry cut in half.

COUPE LIEGEOISE

- chocolate sauce
- vanilla bean ice cream
- real chocolate ice cream
- whipped cream
- wafer biscuit or tuile
- good-quality chocolate, white and dark, to garnish (shavings, cigarettes or grated)
- chocolate croquante (crunchy biscuit pieces in chocolate)

Place some chocolate sauce in the bottom of a glass, one as eccentric as possible. Add 3 scoops of ice cream in either combination. Top with whipped cream and garnish with more chocolate sauce, a wafer biscuit or tuile, the chocolate garnish and chocolate croquante.

KIOSK ◆ BILLETTERIE

At the bottom of the stairs is a large foyer that reminds me of a cinema, with a mural celebrating the freedom and excitement of travel and the nostalgia of that time when you just manage to miss a train. On your right is a pair of doors. They might have a red rope outside. There may be a small and wittily exclamatory poster to advertise some joy to come. If you're here during the daytime the room will be empty. It has small tables and chairs facing a low stage. It'll probably hold a dozing grand piano. At the back of the room is a bar and above the bar an elaborate clock with

a pair of roosters squaring up to each other in neon. This is The Crazy Coqs cabaret bar.

Cabaret is a rare entertainment in London. Of all the things that were stifled by mass entertainment – the stadium and the internet – cabaret was the most vulnerable. It's usually now found in the neutered walk-through spaces of grand hotels, where endangered pianists rattle off standard Las Vegas ballads for drunk stop-overs and businessmen seducing their personal assistants. Real cabaret can be the most intense and intimate experience; singers and songs that reach you not as a collective amplified experience but a shared one – like a cultural pheromone. In the evening, in the dark, the waiters bus the tables like questing meerkats. The room becomes electric with anticipation and emotion. Cabaret isn't passive, it's not something that you sit back and let wash over you: the audience is part of the process. At its best it feels like a collaboration.

The word 'cabaret' comes from the old French for a tap room. A vaulted room. It's the idea of entertainment whilst you drink and eat that is particularly French. The great inspiration of cabaret came from *fin-de-siècle* Paris. We know the very first ever purpose-built, fully-crafted cabaret – a café with entertainment. It was made by Rodolphe Salis at 84 Boulevard Rochechouart. He wanted a place where working men, bohemians, artists and writers could drink Absinthe in the style of Louis XIV. The decoration never amounted to much more than a fireplace ornamented by the bust of said Louis as a young boy. The place was called Le Chat Noir. There is a famous poster advertising it which you can find in Zédel, on the stairs going down. Resplendent, gold-covered Swiss Guards stood at the door to welcome artists and writers and keep out priests and the military. What really made the Black Cat a success was the noisy arrival of Emile Goudeau and his collective of radical writers who called themselves the Hydropathes. This was a literary drinking club where the name indicated the morbid fear of water. It met weekly and drunkenly to declaim and declare and recite poetry. Emile Goudeau would pay his contributors with drink. He was a proselytising advocate of wormwood Absinthe that was to become the defining drug of the age, both demonised and romanticised – it could either blind or illuminate. The Hydropathes decamped to the Black Cat, produced a monthly magazine, sang songs, danced and inadvertently invented disco. Rodolphe Salis was an imposing man with dyed red hair and beard, florid waistcoat and a deep hectoring voice that was, it was said, full of cynicism (how could they tell in Paris?). He would harangue the smart and fashionable for slumming it with the dangerous and attractive working class in Montmartre.

The idea and the driving energy of cabaret were undeniably, indisputably, political. From the street. And it came with a new dance – the Apache.

Toulouse-Lautrec

'La Goulue' (Louise Weber)

JANE
Avril

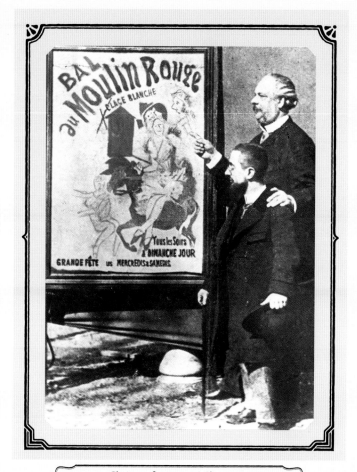

Toulouse-Lautrec and Tremolada

This was taken from the poorest dives in the slums and revitalised with a melodramatic passion. It was the dance of a prostitute with her pimp. It is choreographed domestic abuse, a fight of slaps and punches, hair pulling and feigned unconsciousness. It says something about Paris in the 1890s and the irony of the newly-intellectual class that this could be seen as artistic rather than delinquent. The name Apache came from the excessively violent gangs of criminals who roamed the streets at night and called themselves after the Penny Dreadful depictions of American Indians – Apaches, the mercilessly cunning and cruel murderers. The Apache Dance was mocked and mimicked around the world, put in the movies by D.W. Griffith and silent comedies by Charlie Chaplin and Tom and Jerry. It seemed to encapsulate the extremes and absurdity of French culture. The other dance that is synonymous with cabaret is the can-can (the 'scandal'), originally named after the group of dancers called Clodoches, and now you can't see it without hearing Offenbach's infernal gallop. It started as an energetic and acrobatic dance for couples – again in working class dance halls – and was often danced by men. Indeed an all-male troupe called the Quadrille des Clodoches came to London. The dance became the totem of the energy and sexuality of Paris, its public daring and the surrender to pleasure. Two women made can-can famous – both of them painted by Toulouse-Lautrec. Louise Weber was a Jewish girl who came, like so much café culture, from Alsace-Lorraine. She danced at the Moulin Rouge and invented many of the steps that are associated with the chorus dance, kicking the hats off men in the audience. She got the nickname La Goulue – the glutton – for draining the glasses as she danced past tables. La Goulue became the highest paid entertainer in France and she left the Moulin at the height of her fame to take her show on the road with a circus. Naturally, with typical tragedy, she lost all her money, took to drink, got fat and ended her days anonymously selling peanuts and matches outside the café theatre where she had once kept audiences rapt. The girl who took over from her was Jane Avril, also Jewish – the illegitimate child of a prostitute and, apocryphally, a purported aristocrat. She was abused as a child and put into an asylum suffering from 'Saint Vitus Dance', was treated for female hysteria and discovered that Terpsichore was her escape and cure. She became the lead can-can dancer. Her style, they said, was markedly different to the Clodoches', which had been energetic, expansive and affectionate. Jane Avril was elegant, aloof and untouchably erotic. She is the muse for Nicole Kidman's character in *Moulin Rouge*. She was also feted and fornicated with before leaving to marry a German artist who, of course, tragically cheated on her, drank and disappeared for weeks on end. Avril died quietly and sadly in an old people's home in Paris in 1943 whilst the Germans filled the cabarets and cafés. Tragedy, it turns out, is an important element in the *mise-en-scène* of French cabaret. The brief, intense love in the spotlight that is granted to art is often born out of hardship and sadness – and that's where it will return. Cabaret came from the streets, from working class lives that were forged in disappointment. The stage was a moment of glory and beauty, but its price was always too high. This working class understanding of lost love and dashed hopes makes the emotion and the passion so intense. The most famous of all cabaret artists was Edith Piaf – *La Môme Piaf* – whose story was the archetype of Parisian tragedy. She, too, was brought up in a brothel. Named after Edith Cavell, the English nurse executed by the Germans for helping French soldiers, as a child Piaf went blind and her sight was restored by the hookers with hearts who sent her on a pilgrimage for a miracle. Her only child died of meningitis, and her love life was a series of famous and public train wrecks, except for her gentle boxer, who died in a plane crash before he

Maurice Chevalier and Mistinguett

could beat the music out of her like everyone else. So of course, he remained the love of her life. Piaf's 'Non, Je Ne Regrette Rien' was the anthem of cabaret. But it was Piaf's last lines gasped as she died of cancer in 1963 that could be the motto of her admiring, empathising audience. 'Every damn fool thing you do in this life you pay for.'

Maurice Chevalier, the famous comic musical singer who became Hollywood's idea of a Frenchman and sang 'Sanc 'evan for leetle girls', a particularly unsavoury number, got his break by having a brief affair with a great French chanteuse called Fréhel who looked like a prop forward in a Henry-V wig. Having got his leg over and up, he dumped her for the even more famous Mistinguett. Fréhel attempted suicide, but of course failed. She hit the bottle, moved to Russia and came back after ten years to be an utterly titanic star, plainly having stocked up on a lifetime's tragedy. She sang a type of music called *bal musette*, which had originally come from Italy and was popular in low bohemian dives, and it gave us the greatest cultural timbre that Paris café life has to answer for – the accordion. Like the banjo and the mouth-organ, the accordion has all the appurtenances of a musical instrument without ever producing anything you would actually call music, but it became the unavoidable sound of the city. What sirens are to New York, gypsy violins to Budapest, car horns to Rome, the comic wheezing of the accordion is to Paris.

It was the war that proved to be the swan song and the defining moment of cabaret. Paris was an open city, excused by the war, too precious to European culture to be bombed. But also the great prize of war. For the Nazis it was the capital of their traditional enemy and the city where a united Germany had been proclaimed two generations earlier. But Paris represented so many things that Berlin wasn't. Hitler's triumphant visit was a dynamic moment in the war, lovingly recorded by the Germans. The politics, the emotion and the tragedy embodied in cabaret are evident in two contrasting fictional observations: one in *Goodbye to Berlin*, Christopher Isherwood's memoir of pre-war Nazi Berlin where the memorable Sally Bowles emerges as an international lost version of Piaf who inspires the musical *Cabaret*; and in *Casablanca*, Rick's Café, an idealised and deeply romanticised vision of occupied France where the Germans start to sing their martial oom-pah-pah songs and a fragile French chanteuse stands to clearly offer 'The Marseillaise'. The cowed and desperate Free French join in, eventually drowning out the bosh. It is apocryphal and sentimental, but it does tap the essential struggle of cabaret during the war. Many stars stayed in Paris and continued to perform for audiences of both occupying Germans and French. There were accusations of collaboration against Maurice Chevalier and Edith Piaf, who claimed to have secretly worked for the Resistance.

Someone else who stayed in Paris and did work for the Deuxième Bureau was Josephine Baker. She had come over with the Revue Nègre and danced and sang and performed burlesque at the Folies Bergère.

Jazz arrived in Paris with American troops in the last year of the First World War. It coincided with and fuelled an interest in African culture amongst writers and artists: Picasso, Stravinsky and Apollinaire all used African rhythms and images. It was Fernand Léger who suggested bringing over an African-American act. Josephine Baker was the inevitably illegitimate daughter of a singer and an absent drummer and was said to be half black and half Indian. She was wholly sensational; a sophisticated and syncopated modern dancer who grew to become an equally brilliant singer. The Revue Nègre in Paris was seen as authentic black culture, although in truth it was a projection of white avant-garde exoticism and eroticism.

Josephine Baker

VEDETTE
Columbia 🎵
LINE VIALA

It did mean that black performers could work more freely with greater warmth and acceptance in Paris than they ever could in America. Baker also worked for the Resistance throughout the war, often at great personal danger. Her reputation meant she could travel freely. She really did go to Casablanca carrying secret messages in her knickers in support of the Free French. After the victory she was given the Croix de Guerre and made a 'chevalier' of the Légion d'honneur. She returned to America but there Americans didn't see a sophisticated, strong American black woman with all the panache, glamour and culture of Paris – it was intimidating and humiliating. She was replaced as Gypsy Rose Lee in the musical, but continued to visit America to support civil rights beside Martin Luther King dressed in her Free French uniform. She was the first black woman to star in a film – *Zouzou* in 1934. But this being cabaret, of course, it all ended badly. A string of divorces and unsuccessful love affairs – with both genders – unpaid bills and bankruptcy; but finally, too late, she played to a standing ovation at Carnegie Hall and died in bed in a flat that was lent to her by Grace Kelly in Monaco. She is the only American woman to be buried with full French military honours – but then she wasn't really American, or French... She belonged to cabaret. The Revue Nègre led to a strong and enduring connection between black performers and cabaret. The style, the anger, the neediness and the emotion were a perfect fit for generations of black singers and dancers who found their voices in the smoky-dark with a microphone and a small band singing intimately to invisible couples at tables. The legacy of Apache music found echoes in jazz – the need to tell a story – hard, passionate lives craving the group hug of the rooms. Ernest Hemingway said with customary absolutism that Josephine Baker was the most sensational woman anyone had ever seen – and that will do as an obituary.

Hemingway notoriously liberated the bar at the Ritz in 1944 in an act of bravado that has gone down in journalistic mythology. The truth was rather more prosaic. The Ritz didn't need liberating. Hermann Göring who'd had a suite there had already packed his many lady-boy frocks and departed, but Hemingway was desperate to be part of it and stole a commission from another journalist to follow Patton into France. The other hack was, unfortunately, his wife Martha Gellhorn – a much better journalist, but not a patch on him as a tall storyteller. Hemingway, middle-aged, overweight and drunk, dressed up in a uniform and attracted a group of French partisans – mostly with a great many bottles of Champagne – also a couple of military historians. He commandeered a motorcycle and sidecar, strapped on a pistol that he'd liberated from the corpse of a Prussian – it bore the motto 'Gott mit uns' (God with us), which presumably, for the original owner should have been 'Uns mit Gott' – and anyway, it was against every rule and convention in journalism to be armed. He led his irregulars unsteadily through the backstreets of Paris stopping at the Travellers Club and a couple of other bars for Champagne, before tipping up at the back door of the Ritz, where the nervous manager let him in on condition that he left the gun at the door and ushered the great, addled, fat fantasist into the small bar that now bears his name. The management had every reason to be nervous – the Ritz was the only hotel the Nazis had allowed to stay open and the staff were terrified of being strung up from their own chandeliers. They told papa Hemingway that they'd been working for the Resistance and as proof pointed out the finest vintages that had been hidden at great personal cost. Hemingway was satisfied and drank Montrachet like a kid drinks soda.

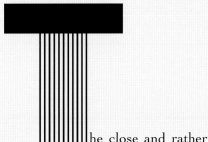

The close and rather complicated bond of Americans and the Parisian Grand Café is acknowledged in the American Bar at Zédel. Too dark in which to read *A Moveable Feast*, but a perfect room in which to tell stories of liberation and bravado. A place devoted to cocktails before they were infantilised with *double entendre* and enough syrup to blanket the essential grown-up pleasure of hard liquor. The origin of cocktails is murky, as you might imagine. People who can't remember where they were last night are unlikely to remember if they invented a cocktail. They are almost certainly American. One of the first nineteenth-century references is to a bittered sling, a drink much used in electioneering by democrats, 'for if you could swallow it you would swallow anything'. We don't know what the first cocktail was made of or by whom, but we do know when the first cocktail party was thrown. It was in St. Louis, Missouri in May 1917. The *St. Paul Pioneer Press* wrote: 'Positively the newest thing in society is the giving of cocktail parties'. The trailblazer was given by Mrs Josephine Dickson Walsh, wife of Julius Walsh, owner of four railways and a bank. Josephine was the arbiter of social matters in St. Louis, so after church one Sunday, fifty swanky Missourians trooped up to the Walsh mansion (which sported its own bar) for mixed drinks. The party lasted an hour and was finished for lunch... although the *St. Paul Pioneer Press* rather spoils the swanky atmosphere by calling it dinner. Josephine Dickson Walsh had form when it came to inventing alcoholic social events. I discovered that she had previously arranged a 'baby party' at the St. Louis Country Club where guests were invited to dress up as toddlers and drink, or rather suck, alcohol from babies' bottles. I think it's fair to say that Mrs Dickson Walsh must have been something of a social caution, and it's only with a serendipitous good luck for civilisation that it was the cocktail party and not the toddler bash which caught on and took over the world. The cocktail party was imported to England, not as some think by Alec Waugh, Evelyn's feyer brother who wrote the lad-loving *The Loom of Youth*, but by Christopher Nevinson, the war artist who was searching for something to do between lunch and dinner. What cocktails were actually served at the first bash in St. Louis? Well apparently the Bronx Gin: dry vermouth, sweet vermouth and orange and clover leaves; gin, grenadine lime juice and egg white garnished with mint. One lady, chilled from motoring in her open limo, warmed herself with something called a Sazerac – whiskey, sugar and bitters in a glass washed with Absinthe. Sazerac is the name of a Kentucky bourbon distilling company. It may be that the Sazerac is the oldest cocktail in America, pre-dating the Civil War. I think the American Bar should resurrect it and every so often raise a toast to Josephine Dickson Walsh in appreciation of her great invention. It's very hard to come up with a new social occasion – most of them were old hat before the birth of Aristotle – but the cocktail party is one. And it wasn't just a new space, place and time to eat and drink, but it also ushered in a new way of talking – cocktail party chat. It's as formulaic as the formal responses in church. And the cocktail party became the leitmotif of the capitalist twentieth century. The triumph of style over content. You don't have to be clever, talented, pretty or even interesting to navigate a cocktail party. The drinks themselves make up for all the deficiencies of the drinkers.

American bars are more French than they are American. I doubt there are many bars in America called the American Bar, but there are quite a lot in France. One of the first things that made Paris's Grand Café life so splendid in the 100 years before the Paris Commune and the second war was that Paris became such an international city. Café society was made up in great part by immigrants who had no other part of society to belong to. Established families and businesses in Paris had each other and their houses to entertain in. It was the world that was either drawn to the liberty and opportunity in Paris or whose people had been thrown out of their own homes who were the habitués of the café. The first to actively attract ex-pats – and in particular Anglophone ones – was Le Dôme in Montparnasse. Now it's a fish restaurant. But it was so successful it also attracted a lot of competitors that formed the vertebrae of the Left Bank down which the nervous system of a new century's avant-garde talked, thought and sparkled. La Rotonde, mentioned in *The Sun Also Rises*, is where Gertrude Stein spilt wine

Humphrey Bogart, Lauren Bacall and Josephine Baker at the Café de Paris, London

over Scott Fitzgerald possibly igniting the idea of a scene in a book where there are lots and lots of clean shirts. Where T.S. Eliot sat musing on whether he should be American and therefore modern or European and therefore intellectual and whether or not he dare eat a peach. He did all three. The Dingo Bar, set up in 1923 specifically to attract English-speaking clientele – this is where Fitzgerald and Hemingway held a famous pissing contest to settle an argument about manliness. Fitzgerald won by an inch, but Hemingway complained that the 'Great Gatsby' had cheated by having more ammunition. Here Nancy Cunard practised being dolorous, erotic and intellectual – all at the same time. Nancy should perhaps be the patron saint of café life. She shagged almost everyone worth talking to and added on a few who weren't but were just pretty. She wore huge African bangles up her arms to hide the needle marks and supported Africans and the avant-garde alternative way of looking at art, decoration and culture. People laughed at her and then copied her and then Parisian jewellers made savage jewellery fashionable and expensive and in a blissfully French way missed the point. Nancy had a longish affair with Henry Crowder, a black jazz player. She became a life-long activist for equal rights, writing a novel called *Negro* and a pamphlet entitled *Black Man and White Ladyship*, exploring prejudice, in which she quoted her own mother as saying: 'Is it true that my daughter knows a negro?'. She ran supplies to the Republicans during the Spanish Civil War and outed Evelyn Waugh as a supporter of Franco. Her personal publishing house printed all the poets and writers she had shagged and a few she had not got round to yet, like Beckett and Pound. She was magnificent. And of course, in the way of all café life, tragic. Went bonkers. And died weighing no more than a hungry Chihuahua. She was cremated in England but they sent back her ashes in a matchbox and she is interred in Père Lachaise, the cemetery of marvellous tragedy.

Harry's Bar

Café de Flore

The final backroom snug of café society here was Harry's New York Bar, named after its manager who was Scots and brought in ex-pats including Sinclair Lewis, Humphrey Bogart and inevitably Hemingway. And there was La Coupole, which is still there and something of a tourist attraction for Americans who want to sit where earlier Americans have sat and write home about America. It was set up in 1927 to emulate Le Dôme and was a favourite of Simone de Beauvoir and Jean-Paul Sartre. La Closerie was much older and opened its doors in 1847, the year Edison, Graham Bell and Bram Stoker were born. It was here that Gertrude Stein berated the omnipresent Hemingway for being in three or four cafés at once and Henry James might have met Leon Trotsky which, if it isn't already a play by Terence Rattigan, damn well ought to be one by David Hare. Incidentally, at the same time, a man called Ramón Mercader was drinking cocktails at Café de Flore. A few years later, he travelled to Mexico with a barman's ice-pick and stabbed Trotsky in the head with it. Café de Flore held an annual literary festival offering a small cash prize and offered to the winner a glass of Pouilly Fumé every day for a year. I am trying to persuade Zédel to consider taking that up. The Deux Magots also had an annual literary award and it goes without saying that Hemingway was an habitual barfly with Rimbaud, André Gide, Picasso, Sartre, de Beauvoir, Vargas, Loyola and everyone else who was trying to keep out of Nancy Cunard's bed for a couple of days.

The fact that so much Grand Café life in France was practised by non-Frenchmen doesn't make it any less French, or rather Parisian. Artists, writers, heiresses, egotists, fantasists, eroticists, remittance men and exoto-philes all gravitated to Paris because they could find or make the sort of society that didn't exist anywhere else in Europe and therefore the world. That was definingly French but created by people who weren't – anything but.

SAZERAC

crushed ice and ice cubes

30ml rye whiskey

30ml Cognac

2 dashes of Angostura bitters

2 dashes of Peychaud's Bitters

3ml Absinthe

lemon zest, to garnish

EQUIPMENT

old-fashioned glass

mixing glass, bar spoon, atomiser
and julep strainer

Chill the old-fashioned glass with crushed ice and water.

Put the rye whiskey, Cognac and bitters into a mixing glass and stir with a bar spoon.

Discard the crushed ice and water from the old-fashioned glass. Spray the inside of the glass with the Absinthe using an atomiser.

Pour the contents of the mixing glass into the old-fashioned and add ice cubes. Add the lemon zest.

BOULEVARDIER

25ml bourbon

25ml Campari

25ml sweet vermouth

ice cubes (optional)

orange twist, to garnish (optional)

EQUIPMENT

mixing glass, bar spoon and julep strainer

champagne flute or old-fashioned glass

Put the bourbon, Campari and sweet vermouth into a mixing glass. Stir with a bar spoon.

Strain through a julep strainer and into a champagne flute.

For a punchier alternative, serve in an old-fashioned glass over ice, with an orange twist.

Meanwhile, upstairs in Zédel's café bar, people off the street come to sit and take the weight off, read the paper before their next appointment, and meet a friend. I was last there to meet my nephew – a boy who lives in a world of cafés. Cafés are where we meet people and where we go to be alone; they're convivial and solitary, they're not age specific and, because of their origins in Paris and the classes and colours who made them, they are completely non-judgemental about who you are, where you come from, who you sleep with or pray to. The café first served the coffee that came out of the Queen of Sheba's incense forests in Ethiopia, collected by Yemenis. It was given a roof in Ottoman Turkey and picked up and made over in mercantile Catholic Italy and analysing Austria. Banking, insurance, investment and commercial credit were invented in Protestant London cafés. In Paris it took refugees from Alsace and in the age of European revolutions and republicanism its customers and waiters came from Spain, Greece, Italy, Russia, Scandinavia, Ireland, Scotland and the Americas... from the Maghreb and Sub-Saharan Africa. Those escaping their families, their religion, prejudice and dogma – gay people, black people, half-black, half-gay, half-mad people. People who wanted to live different lives, sing different songs, write new stories, construct new philosophies... Every Communist and Anarcho-Syndicalist would be served by an orthodox Count or a fleeing royalist. Without cafés there would be no modern jazz, no Cubism, no Dada, no new-wave cinema, no dialectic,

no stream of consciousness, no existentialism, post-structuralism, modernism or post-modernism – and if there were, they wouldn't be the same or remotely as exciting or amusing. But all of this is to really miss the bigger point – the true grandness of the Grand Café. It wasn't about the fraction of customers who would write the great American novel, compose an atonal symphony or a smoky ballad, draw a lover, write blank verse for a lost love or take a black and white snap... It was for the thousands and thousands of clerks and shop assistants, the drivers and students, civil servants and the people who spend their lives on their feet in cheap shoes behind someone else's desk, those who lifted things, pushed things, did repetitive, dangerous, thankless things or did nothing. Had no one. The café was their country, their escape, a place where they could eat good food at an affordable price; sit and nurse a *pichet* of wine; take a paper from the rack, watch the world. They could have their picture taken by Doisneau; be local colour in a Camus novel or poem by Verlaine; they could hear Piaf sing to a drunken soldier; see Chevalier do a soft shoe shuffle; could have their elbow jogged by that insufferable bore Hemingway. The grandness of Grand Cafés was not that they offered a haven for the talented or the proto-famous, but that they offered the same refuge and rough respect to the perfectly ordinary.

Tom Paine the English-American exile, one time corset-maker, journalist and profound pamphleteer and bloody marvellous awkward sod, lived for a time in Paris during the revolution. He was imprisoned by Robespierre. He wrote in the newly-invented cafés the most widely-read, non-religious book ever made. In it is said that men need governments and laws for the things they can't agree amongst themselves. Government is not a mark of our success as a society, but the consequence of our failure as people. True to the curse of the café, having helped create a nation, Paine died ridiculed and shunned by virtually everyone. There were six mourners at his funeral: a woman and her son – he had been paying for the boy's education; a Quaker on a horse who disapproved of him but didn't want him to go to his grave alone; a vicar; and two black men who were just grateful to him. The café is the shining example of Paine's truth. It is not made by law or dictated by government or tradition, it isn't created by faith or politics, it is the thing we came up with by ourselves, for ourselves. A decent, amusing, moveable, funny, exciting, gentle, repeatable place to be solo or sociable in. It's a triumph of inclusive culture and collectively-constructed civilisation. Forgiving of weakness and as comfortable with failure as success, a balm for sadness, a stage for joy, a library, a podium and a studio for creativity – as well as a carafe for politics and a sauceboat for change. The grandness of the café is a memorial to the best of us.

INDEX

Pages in *italics* refer to
illustrations

Publishing Director	Sarah Lavelle
Creative Director	Helen Lewis
Senior Editor	Céline Hughes
Designer	Lawrence Morton
Photographer	David Loftus
Production	Vincent Smith, Steve McCabe

First published in 2016 by Quadrille Publishing, Pentagon House, 52–54 Southwark Street London SE1 1UN
www.quadrille.co.uk

Quadrille is an imprint of Hardie Grant
www.hardiegrant.com.au

Narrative text © 2016 A.A. Gill

Recipe text © 2016 Corbin & King

Photography © 2016 David Loftus, except pages listed below

Design and layout © 2016 Quadrille Publishing

Cataloguing in Publication Data: a catalogue record for this book is available from the British Library.

Hardback ISBN: 978 184949 4670
Paperback ISBN: 978 184949 7954

Printed in China

Picture credits

Page 1, Le Dôme Café, Montparnasse, Paris. 1928. Andre Kertesz

Pages 2, 4, 6–7, 23, 30, 34–37, 39, 40, 43, 45, 46, 49 (left), 50, 53, 55, 57, 59, 60, 63, 65, 67, 69, 70, 73, 74, 77, 79, 80, 83, 84 (right), 89, 91, 93, 94, 97, 98 (right), 100, 103, 104–5, 107, 118, 119 (left), 122-123, 133–136, David Loftus

Pages 9, 10, London Metropolitan Archives, City of London

Page 26, Corbis

Page 16, (left) FPG/Getty Images; (right) Robert DOISNEAU/Gamma-Rapho/Getty Images

Page 17, (left) Photo by Roger Viollet/Getty Images; (right) Robert DOISNEAU/Gamma-Rapho/Getty Images

Pages 49 (right); 84 (left); 98 (left); 119 (right), A C Cooper

Page 110 (left), Roger-Viollet/REX Shutterstock; (right) adoc-photos/Corbis

Page 111 (left), Corbis; (right) Henry Guttmann/Getty Images

Page 114 (main), KEYSTONE-FRANCE/Getty Images; (inset) Corbis

Page 117 (left), George Hoyningen-Huene © Condé Nast Archive/Corbis; (right) © RA/Lebrecht Music & Arts

Page 124, © Lebrecht/Lebrecht Music & Arts

Page 128, John Heddon/Express/Getty Images

Page 130 (left), Sabine WEISS/RAPHO/Getty Images; (right) Keystone-France/Getty Images

Page 144 Fox Photos/Getty Images

ACKNOWLEDGEMENTS

It is so important to thank Michele Klepper, Adrian's amanuensis for all her text work, and of course the estimable Nicola Formby who tested and checked all the recipes.

At Brasserie Zédel, Executive Chef Andrew Parkinson was responsible for writing the recipes, assisted by Chefs Jana Muller and Stuart Lane together with pâtissiers D'Arcy Demerse and Joyzanne Pereira; Bar Manager Michael Browne for the cocktails; Laura Sebag-Montefiore for the organising; and Robert Holland for corralling them all. Jacqui Black found the historical photos, and of course David Loftus's contemporary photos are peerless.

We are in awe of Céline Hughes, our editor at Quadrille, as well as the most intuitive and brilliant of designers, Lawrence Morton; they both made the experience so much easier... Ed Victor for cajoling us both and Alison Cathie who believes in this book so much she was prepared to put her money where her mouth was and has a running bet on it.

A.A.Gill & J.R.B. King